Advanced Care Planning:

Crafting Your Healthcare & Financial Decisions

Glenda Walsh Crouse, CEOLD

This is not a legally binding document. It is meant to organize the client's wishes regarding their healthcare when they are not able to speak for themselves. You have permission to photocopy **completed** pages of this document to distribute to family, friends and medical care teams to notify them of your clients final wishes, with permission of the client only and within HIPPA requirements. **ACP forms are for the State of <u>Maryland </u>and are included for reference**. Forms can be printed for free from my website. After completing official forms, keep them in this booklet to organize and make sure your preferences are clear. Feel free to contact me with suggestions for content. Additional end of life planning resources also available on the website.

www.glendawalshcrouse.com

Table of Contents

Agent

Who can you rely on to carry out your wishes and speak for you if you can't speak for yourself? What is their contact information?

____

____

____

____

____

____

____

- ❏ I have notified this individual.
- ❏ I have discussed my wishes with this individual.
- ❏ I have provided copies of paperwork and wishes to this individual.

Where are your Advanced Care Directive/Documents located?

____

____

____

____

____

____

____

Beliefs

What values, experiences, faith or beliefs influence your choices?

$C$are Goals

Where do you want to be? Home, hospital, other medical facility?

What support systems do you currently have in place?

What does quality of life mean to you?

What additional support might be needed?

____

____

____

____

____

____

What's the next step if this plan doesn't work out?

Plan A

____

____

____

____

____

____

____

____

Plan B

____

____

____

____

____

____

____

Plan C

Other notes:

Advanced Care Planning Forms

The following forms are documents needed in the **State of Maryland**. The documents pictured are for reference purposes. You can print copies of these documents on my website www.glendawalshcrouse.com or www.marylandmolst.org/.

Maryland Law permits **Advanced Directives** to be completed on paper, a video, another electronic document or online. The printable document referenced in this book can be printed free on my website or here:

www.marylandattorneygeneral.gov/Pages/HealthPolicy/advancedirectives.aspx

Complete your Advanced Directive **electronically** here: www.mydirectives.com/

Printable Advanced Directive **wallet cards** can be found on my website or here:

www.marylandattorneygeneral.gov/Health%20Policy%20Documents/adDir_cards.pdf

Health Care Decision Making Worksheet

Instructions

Use this worksheet to indicate current treatment preferences (which will be reflected in Maryland MOLST orders) or to clarify wishes for future situations (which will be applied only when the issues become relevant in the future). Only initial those items for which a decision has been made or is needed. The remaining items can be left blank.

Although the choices on this worksheet represent wishes regarding various life-sustaining treatment options, this is not an order sheet or an advance directive. For example, preferences about artificially administered fluids and nutrition would be incorporated into current orders if the individual currently has impaired nutrition or fluid/electrolyte balance that cannot be corrected in another way. On the other hand, if the individual is eating or drinking adequately and related problems are not anticipated in the near future, then orders related to limiting these treatments may not need to be entered on the MOLST form. It may still be appropriate to do so if the individual has definitely decided about these treatments for the future and has been fully informed about the risks and benefits of those treatments in all the various situations that may arise. The individual should be counselled to prepare an advance directive if the potential treatments at issue are not relevant to the individual's current condition.

Make one choice for cardiopulmonary resuscitation, by initialing the appropriate line. If no choice is made, resuscitation will be attempted by default. Choose one option for each of the other categories, as appropriate and desired, by initialing the appropriate line. Clarify specific care instructions, as needed.

Part A, Main goal(s) of care: Specific treatment preferences should reflect the main goal or goals of care. In Part A, the patient or the patient's authorized decision maker may identify goals of care. It allows for the identification of more than one main goal of care. Often, two goals can be pursued at the same time – for example, prolonging life while controlling pain and other distressing symptoms. But if the use of a life-sustaining treatment would be inconsistent with maximum comfort, as sometimes happens, then health care providers should know which goal is more important.

If the patient lacks capacity, the main goal(s) of care should be identified from the patient's perspective, based on the authorized decision maker's understanding of the patient's wishes, if known, or the patient's best interests. The authorized decision maker's personal beliefs and values should not override those of the patient, even if he or she is an appointed health care agent.

If there are multiple surrogate decision makers of equal authority involved in the preparation of the Health Care Decision Making Worksheet, they may not all agree on a life-sustaining treatment. Or, even if they agree, the attending physician may consider that the identified main goal of care is unrealistic or, if pursued, would result in burdens with little or no benefit for the patient. A health care provider should follow its customary procedures for addressing such conflicts, including, as appropriate, referral to the facility's patient care advisory (ethics) committee.

Part B, Advance directive and authorized decision maker contact information: The Health Care Decision Making Worksheet is not an advance directive or an order form. If a patient has already completed an advance directive, this worksheet could be attached to it. If the advance directive names a health care agent, contact information for the health care agent should be inserted. If there is no health care agent, contact information for the guardian or surrogate decision maker should be inserted. Even if the patient still has capacity, the contact information for whoever is to serve as authorized decision maker after loss of capacity should be included.

HEALTH CARE DECISION MAKING WORKSHEET

<table>
<tr><td colspan="2">Patient's name</td><td>Date of Birth</td><td></td></tr>
<tr><td colspan="2"></td><td></td><td>☐ Male   ☐ Female</td></tr>
<tr><td>Part A

____
Initial this line</td><td colspan="3">Most Important Goal(s) of Care: What does the patient or authorized decision maker hope to achieve?</td></tr>
<tr><td>Part B</td><td colspan="3">If the patient has a written advance directive check this box ☐ and attach a copy.

If the patient currently lacks the capacity to make health care decisions, check this box ☐.

In case the patient lacks or loses capacity, the following individual will make decisions:

Name _________________________   Phone Number _________________________

☐ Health Care Agent   ☐ Guardian   ☐ Surrogate Decision Maker</td></tr>
</table>

	Meanings and Implications
1	**CPR Status:** What should be done to try to prevent or manage an actual or impending cardiopulmonary arrest?

_________ Attempt CPR, Comprehensive Cardiopulmonary Resuscitation Efforts
- If cardiac and/or pulmonary arrest occurs, attempt cardiopulmonary resuscitation (CPR).
- CPR will include comprehensive medical efforts to try to restore and/or stabilize heart and lung function and prevent arrest, including any form of artificial ventilation.

_________ No CPR, Option A-1, Intubate, Comprehensive Efforts to Prevent Arrest, Including Intubation
- If cardiac and/or pulmonary arrest occurs, resuscitation should not be attempted (No CPR). Allow death to occur naturally.
- In order to try to prevent cardiopulmonary arrest, use comprehensive efforts to try to stabilize and/or restore heart and lung function, including intubation where indicated.

_________ No CPR, Option A-2, Do Not Intubate, Comprehensive Efforts to Prevent Arrest, No Intubation
- In order to try to prevent cardiopulmonary arrest, make a comprehensive effort to try to stabilize and/or restore heart and lung function, except for intubation. It is acceptable to use CPAP or BiPAP to try to prevent respiratory failure.
- If cardiac and/or pulmonary arrest occurs, do not attempt resuscitation (No CPR). Allow death to occur naturally.

_________ No CPR, Option B, Palliative and Supportive Care, Palliative and Supportive Care Before and After Cardiopulmonary Arrest
- Do not attempt cardiopulmonary resuscitation (No CPR). Allow death to occur naturally.
- Give supportive measures only, including 1) passive oxygen for comfort, 2) efforts to control any visible bleeding and 3) medications for pain relief.
- Do not attempt to prevent cardiopulmonary arrest. Do not intubate or use CPAP or BiPAP.

	Meanings and Implications
2	**Artificial Ventilation:** What should be done for respiratory failure where cardiopulmonary arrest is not involved?
2a	______ If the patient cannot breathe adequately, the patient may be intubated and put on a ventilator for as long as necessary, even indefinitely.
2b	______ If the patient cannot breathe adequately, the patient may be intubated and put on a ventilator (time limit up to ______ days) to see if the ventilator is effective for a patient's overall condition. If not, stop using the ventilator.
2c	______ If the patient cannot breathe adequately, use only CPAP or BiPAP for a limited time (time limit up to ______ days), to see if it is effective for a patient's overall condition. If not, stop using CPAP or BiPAP . Do not intubate or place on a ventilator other than CPAP or BiPAP.
2d	______ Do not use a ventilator (no intubation, CPAP or BiPAP) under any circumstances.
3	**Blood Transfusion:** Should blood transfusions or infusion of blood products be given?
3a	______ Blood and blood products (whole blood, packed red blood cells, plasma, or platelets) may be given to replace blood products if it is medically indicated.
3b	______ Do not give any blood products.
4	**Hospital Transfers:** Should hospital transfers occur and under what circumstances?
4a	______ Transfer to the hospital is okay for any situation requiring medical care that cannot be given outside of a hospital to diagnose, treat, or monitor the individual.
4b	______ Hospital transfer may occur if necessary for comfort or to relieve severe medical symptoms that cannot be managed elsewhere. Hospitalization should not be used to try to identify, diagnose, and treat or cure underlying causes of symptoms.
4c	______ Do not transfer to a hospital under any circumstances. Assess, treat, and monitor the patient with options available outside of the hospital, as needed and consistent with patient goals.

	Meanings and Implications
5	**Medical Tests**: To what extent should medical tests be performed for diagnosis, treatment, and monitoring?
5a	_________ Any medical tests that are indicated to diagnose, treat, or monitor a patient may be done.
5b	_________ Only perform limited medical tests necessary for symptomatic relief or comfort. Base any needed assessment, diagnosis, treatment, and monitoring on clinical findings rather than tests.
5c	_________ Do not do any medical tests. Base assessment, diagnosis, treatment, and monitoring on clinical findings rather than tests.
6	**Antibiotics**: When should antibiotics be given and to what extent?
6a	_________ Any antibiotics (oral, intravenous, or intramuscular injection) that are medically indicated may be used, by any route of administration, to try to treat an infection.
6b	_________ Oral antibiotics may be used, if medically indicated, to treat an infection. Do not use intravenous or intramuscular antibiotics.
6c	_________ Oral antibiotics may be used if needed to try to relieve symptoms or for comfort, but not with the main goal of trying to cure an infection. Do not use intravenous or intramuscular antibiotics.
6d	_________ Do not give antibiotics. In case of an infection, treat the symptoms, such as giving medicines for fever or pain relief.
7	**Artificially administered fluids and nutrition**: Under what circumstances and to what extent should artificially administered fluids and nutrition be given?
7a	_________ Artificially administered fluids and nutrition may be given if medically indicated, even indefinitely, by any available means. For example, such medical interventions may address treatable causes of weight loss and fluid imbalances.
7b	_________ Artificially administered fluids and nutrition may be given, if indicated, on a trial basis for a limited time (time limit: up to _______ days) to determine if the underlying causes of weight loss can be corrected. Artificially administered fluids and nutrition may also be given for comfort, if consistent with the patient's goals and wishes.
7c	_________ Artificially administered hydration (intravenous or subcutaneous fluids or fluids through a PEG tube) may be given, but not artificial nutrition.
7d	_________ No artificially administered fluids and nutrition will be given. Offer food and fluids by mouth as desired and tolerated.

	Meanings and Implications
8	**Dialysis:** When should dialysis be used if the kidneys do not function adequately?
8a	_________ Dialysis (either hemodialysis or peritoneal) may be given, even indefinitely, if the kidneys are not functioning adequately. Dialysis may be used for an acute or chronic kidney problem.
8b	_________ Dialysis (either hemodialysis or peritoneal) that is medically indicated may be given for a limited period (time limit: up to ______ days) to determine if it is effective and warranted based on the patient's condition.
8c	_________ No dialysis should be provided.
9	**Other Treatments:** Are there any other instructions related to life-sustaining treatments not otherwise covered in Sections 1-8 above? _________ Initial this line

<table>
<tr><td>Print patient's name

Signature of patient</td><td>

Date</td></tr>
<tr><td>Print name of authorized decision maker
☐ Health Care Agent   ☐ Guardian   ☐ Surrogate Decision Maker

Signature of authorized decision maker</td><td>

Phone

Date</td></tr>
<tr><td>Print name of health care professional assisting with form

Signature of health care professional assisting with form</td><td>Phone

Date</td></tr>
<tr><td>Print name of patient's physician, nurse practitioner, or physician assistant

Signature of patient's physician, nurse practitioner, or physician assistant</td><td>Phone

Date</td></tr>
</table>

13

Completing the Form: The physician, NP, or PA shall select only 1 choice in Section 1 and only 1 choice in any of the other Sections that apply to this patient. If any of Sections 2-9 do not apply, leave them blank. Use Section 9 to document any other orders related to life-sustaining treatments. The order form is not valid until a physician, NP, or PA signs and dates it. Each page that contains orders must be signed and dated. A copy or the original of every completed MOLST form must be given to a competent patient or authorized decision maker within 48 hours of completion of the form or sooner if the patient is discharged or transferred.

Selecting CPR (Resuscitation) Status: EMS Option A-1 – Intubate, Option A-2 – Do Not Intubate, and Option B include a set of medical interventions. You cannot alter the set of interventions associated with any of these options and cannot override or alter the interventions with orders in Section 9.

> **No-CPR Option A: Comprehensive Efforts to Prevent Cardiac and/or Respiratory Arrest / DNR if Arrest – No CPR. This choice may be made either with or without intubation as a treatment option.** Prior to arrest, all interventions allowed under *The Maryland Medical Protocols for EMS Providers*. Depending on the choice, intubation may or may not be utilized to try to prevent arrest. Otherwise, CPAP or BiPAP will be the only devices used for ventilatory assistance. In all cases, comfort measures will also be provided. No CPR if arrest occurs.

> **No-CPR Option B: Supportive Care Prior to Cardiac and/or Respiratory Arrest. DNR if Arrest Occurs – No CPR.** Prior to arrest, interventions may include opening the airway by non-invasive means, providing passive oxygen, controlling external bleeding, positioning and other comfort measures, splinting, pain medications by orders obtained from a physician (e.g., by phone or electronically), and transport as appropriate. No CPR if arrest occurs.

The DNR A-1, DNR A-2 (DNI) and DNR B options will be authorized by this original order form, a copy or a fax of this form, or a bracelet or necklace with the DNR emblem. EMS providers or medical personnel who see these orders are to provide care in accordance with these orders and the applicable *Maryland Medical Protocols for EMS Providers*. Unless a subsequent order relating to resuscitation has been issued or unless the health care provider reasonably believes a DNR order has been revoked, every health care provider, facility, and program shall provide, withhold, or withdraw treatment according to these orders in case of a patient's impending cardiac or respiratory arrest.

Location of Form: The original or a copy of this form shall accompany patients when transferred or discharged from a facility or program. Health care facilities and programs shall maintain this order form (or a copy of it) with other active medical orders or in a section designated for MOLST and related documents in the patient's active medical record. At the patient's home, this form should be kept in a safe and readily available place and retrieved for responding EMS and health care providers before their arrival. The original, a copy, and a faxed MOLST form are all valid orders. There is no expiration date for the MOLST or EMS DNR orders in Maryland.

Reviewing the Form: These medical orders are based on this individual's current medical condition and wishes. Patients, their authorized decision makers and attending physicians, NPs, or PAs shall review and update, if appropriate, the MOLST orders annually and whenever the patient is transferred between health care facilities or programs, is discharged, has a substantial change in health status, loses capacity to make health care decisions, or changes his or her wishes.

Updating the Form: The MOLST form shall be voided and a new MOLST form prepared when there is a change to any of the orders. If modified, the physician, NP, or PA shall void the old form and complete, sign, and date a new MOLST form.

Voiding the Form: To void this medical order form, the physician, NP, or PA shall draw a diagonal line through the sheet, write "VOID" in large letters across the page, and sign and date below the line. A nurse may take a verbal order from a physician, NP, or PA to void the MOLST order form. Keep the voided order form in the patient's active or archived medical record.

Revoking the Form's DNR Order: In an emergency situation involving EMS providers, the DNR order in Section 1 may be revoked at any time by a competent patient's request for resuscitation made directly to responding EMS providers.

Bracelets and Necklaces: If desired, complete the paper form at the bottom of this page, cut out the bracelet portion below, and place it in a protective cover to wear around the wrist or neck or pinned to clothing. If a metal bracelet or necklace is desired, contact Medic Alert at 1-800-432-5378. Medic Alert requires a copy of this order along with an application to process the request.

How to Obtain This Form: Call 410-706-4367 or go to marylandmolst.org

---

Use of an EMS DNR bracelet is OPTIONAL and at the discretion of the patient or authorized decision maker. Print legibly, have physician, NP, or PA sign, cut off strip, fold, and insert in bracelet or necklace.	☐ DNR A-1 Intubate ☐ DNR A-2 Do Not Intubate ☐ DNR B Pt. Name _________________________ DOB _________ Practitioner Name _________________ Date _________ Practitioner Signature _____________ Phone _________

`*** 3 2013`

Maryland Medical Orders for Life-Sustaining Treatment (MOLST)

Patient's Last Name, First, Middle Initial	Date of Birth	
		☐ Male ☐ Female

This form includes medical orders for Emergency Medical Services (EMS) and other medical personnel regarding cardiopulmonary resuscitation and other life-sustaining treatment options for a specific patient. It is valid in all health care facilities and programs throughout Maryland. This order form shall be kept with other active medical orders in the patient's medical record. The physician, nurse practitioner (NP), or physician assistant (PA) must accurately and legibly complete the form and then sign and date it. The physician, NP, or PA shall select only 1 choice in Section 1 and only 1 choice in any of the other Sections that apply to this patient. If any of Sections 2-9 do not apply, leave them blank. A copy or the original of every completed MOLST form must be given to the patient or authorized decision maker within 48 hours of completion of the form or sooner if the patient is discharged or transferred.

CERTIFICATION FOR THE BASIS OF THESE ORDERS: Mark any and all that apply.

I hereby certify that these orders are entered as a result of a discussion with and the informed consent of:

_________ the patient; or

_________ the patient's health care agent as named in the patient's advance directive; or

_________ the patient's guardian of the person as per the authority granted by a court order; or

_________ the patient's surrogate as per the authority granted by the Heath Care Decisions Act; or

_________ if the patient is a minor, the patient's legal guardian or another legally authorized adult.

Or, I hereby certify that these orders are based on:

_________ instructions in the patient's advance directive; or

_________ other legal authority in accordance with all provisions of the Health Care Decisions Act. All supporting documentation must be contained in the patient's medical records.

_________ Mark this line if the patient or authorized decision maker declines to discuss or is unable to make a decision about these treatments. **The patient's or authorized decision maker's participation in the preparation of the MOLST form is always voluntary. If the patient or authorized decision maker has not limited care, except as otherwise provided by law, CPR will be attempted and other treatments will be given.**

CPR (RESUSCITATION) STATUS: EMS providers must follow the *Maryland Medical Protocols for EMS Providers*.

_________ **Attempt CPR:** If cardiac and/or pulmonary arrest occurs, attempt cardiopulmonary resuscitation (CPR). This will include any and all medical efforts that are indicated during arrest, including artificial ventilation and efforts to restore and/or stabilize cardiopulmonary function.

[If the patient or authorized decision maker does not or cannot make any selection regarding CPR status, mark this option. Exceptions: If a valid advance directive declines CPR, CPR is medically ineffective, or there is some other legal basis for not attempting CPR, mark one of the "No CPR" options below.]

1

No CPR, Option A, Comprehensive Efforts to Prevent Arrest: Prior to arrest, administer all medications needed to stabilize the patient. If cardiac and/or pulmonary arrest occurs, do not attempt resuscitation (No CPR). Allow death to occur naturally.

_________ **Option A-1, Intubate:** Comprehensive efforts may include intubation and artificial ventilation.

_________ **Option A-2, Do Not Intubate (DNI):** Comprehensive efforts may include limited ventilatory support by CPAP or BiPAP, but do not intubate.

_________ **No CPR, Option B, Palliative and Supportive Care:** Prior to arrest, provide passive oxygen for comfort and control any external bleeding. Prior to arrest, provide medications for pain relief as needed, but no other medications. Do not intubate or use CPAP or BiPAP. If cardiac and/or pulmonary arrest occurs, do not attempt resuscitation (No CPR). Allow death to occur naturally.

SIGNATURE OF PHYSICIAN, NURSE PRACTITIONER, OR PHYSICIAN ASSISTANT (Signature and date are required to validate order)

Practitioner's Signature	Print Practitioner's Name	
Maryland License #	Phone Number	Date

15

Orders in Sections 2-9 below do not apply to EMS providers and are for situations other than cardiopulmonary arrest.
Only complete applicable items in Sections 2 through 8, and only select one choice per applicable Section.

2

ARTIFICIAL VENTILATION

2a. _______ May use intubation and artificial ventilation indefinitely, if medically indicated.

2b. _______ May use intubation and artificial ventilation as a limited therapeutic trial.
Time limit____

2c. _______ May use only CPAP or BiPAP for artificial ventilation, as medically indicated.
Time limit____

2d. _______ Do not use any artificial ventilation (no intubation, CPAP or BiPAP).

3

BLOOD TRANSFUSION

3a. _______ May give any blood product (whole blood, packed red blood cells, plasma or platelets) that is medically indicated.

3b. _______ Do not give any blood products.

4

HOSPITAL TRANSFER

4a. _______ Transfer to hospital for any situation requiring hospital-level care.

4b. _______ Transfer to hospital for severe pain or severe symptoms that cannot be controlled otherwise.

4c. _______ Do not transfer to hospital, but treat with options available outside the hospital.

5

MEDICAL WORKUP

5a. _______ May perform any medical tests indicated to diagnose and/or treat a medical condition.

5b. _______ Only perform limited medical tests necessary for symptomatic treatment or comfort.

5c. _______ Do not perform any medical tests for diagnosis or treatment.

6

ANTIBIOTICS

6a. _______ May use antibiotics (oral, intravenous or intramuscular) as medically indicated.

6b. _______ May use oral antibiotics when medically indicated, but do not give intravenous or intramuscular antibiotics.

6c. _______ May use oral antibiotics only when indicated for symptom relief or comfort.

6d. _______ Do not treat with antibiotics.

7

ARTIFICIALLY ADMINISTERED FLUIDS AND NUTRITION

7a. _______ May give artificially administered fluids and nutrition, even indefinitely, if medically indicated.

7b. _______ May give artificially administered fluids and nutrition, if medically indicated, as a trial.
Time limit_________________________

7c. _______ May give fluids for artificial hydration as a therapeutic trial, but do not give artificially administered nutrition.
Time limit_________________________

7d. _______ Do not provide artificially administered fluids or nutrition.

8

DIALYSIS

8a. _______ May give chronic dialysis for end-stage kidney disease if medically indicated.

8b. _______ May give dialysis for a limited period.
Time limit_________________________

8c. _______ Do not provide acute or chronic dialysis.

9

OTHER ORDERS ____
____
____
____
____

SIGNATURE OF PHYSICIAN, NURSE PRACTITIONER, OR PHYSICIAN ASSISTANT (Signature and date are required to validate order)

Practitioner's Signature	Print Practitioner's Name	
Maryland License #	Phone Number	Date

A Guide to

Maryland Law on

Health Care Decisions

(Forms Included)

STATE OF MARYLAND
OFFICE OF THE ATTORNEY GENERAL

Brian E. Frosh
Attorney General

August 2019

Dear Fellow Marylander:

I am pleased to send you an advance directive form that you can use to plan for future health care decisions. The form is *optional*; you can use it if you want or use others, which are just as valid legally. If you have any legal questions about your personal situation, you should consult your own lawyer. If you decide to make an advance directive, be sure to talk about it with those close to you. The conversation is just as important as the document. Give copies to family members or friends and your doctor. Also make sure that, if you go into a hospital, you bring a copy. Please *do not* return completed forms to this office.

Life-threatening illness is a difficult subject to deal with. If you plan now, however, your choices can be respected and you can relieve at least some of the burden from your loved ones in the future. You may also use another enclosed form to make an organ donation or plan for arrangements after death.

Here is some related, important information:

- If you want information about Do Not Resuscitate (DNR) Orders, please visit the website http://marylandmolst.org or contact the Maryland Institute for Emergency Medical Services Systems directly at (410) 706-4367. A Medical Orders for Life-Sustaining Treatment (MOLST) form contains medical orders regarding cardiopulmonary resuscitation (CPR) and other medical orders regarding life-sustaining treatments. A physician or nurse practitioner may use a MOLST form to instruct emergency medical personnel (911 responders) to provide comfort care instead of resuscitation. The MOLST form can be found on the Internet at: http://marylandmolst.org. From that page, click on "MOLST Form."

- The Maryland Department of Health makes available an advance directive focused on preferences about mental health treatment. This can be found on the Internet at: https://bha.health.maryland.gov/Pages/Forms.aspx. From that page, under "Forms," click on "Advance Directive for Mental Health Treatment."

I hope that this information is helpful to you. **I regret that overwhelming demand limits us to supplying one set of forms to each requester.** But please feel free to make as many copies as you wish. Additional information about advance directives can be found on the Internet at:
http://www.oag.state.md.us/healthpol/advancedirectives.htm.

Brian E. Frosh
Attorney General

Your Right To Decide

Adults can decide for themselves whether they want medical treatment. This right to decide - to say yes or no to proposed treatment - applies to treatments that extend life, like a breathing machine or a feeding tube. Tragically, accident or illness can take away a person's ability to make health care decisions. But decisions still have to be made. If you cannot do so, someone else will. These decisions should reflect your own values and priorities.

A Maryland law called the Health Care Decisions Act says that you can do health care planning through "advance directives." An advance directive can be used to name a health care agent. This is someone you trust to make health care decisions for you. An advance directive can also be used to say what your preferences are about treatments that might be used to sustain your life.

The State offers a form to do this planning, included with this pamphlet. The form as a whole is called "Maryland Advance Directive: Planning for Future Health Care Decisions." It has three parts to it: Part I, Selection of Health Care Agent; Part II, Treatment Preferences ("Living Will"); and Part III, Signature and Witnesses. This pamphlet will explain each part.

The advance directive is meant to reflect your preferences. You may complete all of it, or only part, and you may change the wording. You are *not* required by law to use these forms. Different forms, written the way you want, may also be used. For example, one widely praised form, called *Five Wishes,* is available (for a small fee) from the nonprofit organization Aging With Dignity. You can get information about that document from the Internet at www.agingwithdignity.org or write to: Aging with Dignity, P.O. Box 1661, Tallahassee, FL 32302.

This optional form can be filled out without going to a lawyer. But if there is anything you do not understand about the law or your rights, you might want to talk with a lawyer. You can also ask your doctor to explain the medical issues, including the potential benefits or risks to you of various options. You should tell your doctor that you made an advance directive and give your doctor a copy, along with others who could be involved in making these decisions for you in the future.

In Part III of the form, you need two witnesses to your signature. Nearly any adult can be a witness. If you name a health care agent, though, that person may not be a witness. Also, one of the witnesses must be a person who would not financially benefit by your death or handle your estate. You do not need to have the form notarized.

This pamphlet also contains a separate form called "After My Death." Like the advance directive, using it is optional. This form has four parts to it: Part I, Organ Donation; Part II, Donation of Body; Part III, Disposition of Body and Funeral Arrangements; and Part IV, Signature and Witnesses.

Once you make an advance directive, it remains in effect unless you revoke it. It does not expire, and neither your family nor anyone except you can change it. You should review what you've done once in a while. Things might change in your life, or your attitudes might change. You are free to amend or revoke an advance directive at any time, as long as you still have decision-making capacity. Tell your doctor and anyone else who has a copy of your advance directive if you amend it or revoke it.

If you already have a prior Maryland advance directive, living will, or a durable power of attorney for health care, that document is *still valid*. Also, if you made an advance directive in another state, it is valid in Maryland. You might want to review these documents to see if you prefer to make a new advance directive instead.

Part I of the Advance Directive: Selection of Health Care Agent

You can name anyone you want (except, in general, someone who works for a health care facility where you are receiving care) to be your health care agent. **To name a health care agent, use Part I of the advance directive form**. (Some people refer to this kind of advance directive as a "durable power of attorney for health care.") Your agent will speak for you and make decisions based on what you would want done or your best interests. You decide how much power your agent will have to make health care decisions. You can also decide when you want your agent to have this power — right away, or only after a doctor says that you are not able to decide for yourself.

You can pick a family member as a health care agent, but you don't have to. Remember, your agent will have the power to make important treatment decisions, even if other people close to you might urge a different decision. Choose the person best qualified to be your health care agent. Also, consider picking one or two back-up agents, in case your first choice isn't available when needed. Be sure to inform your chosen person and make sure that he or she understands what's most important to you. When the time comes for decisions, your health care agent should follow your written directions.

We have a helpful booklet that you can give to your health care agent. It is called *"Making Medical Decisions for Someone Else: A Maryland Handbook."* You or your agent can get a copy on the Internet at: http://www.marylandattorneygeneral.gov/ Health%20Policy%20Documents/ProxyHan dbook.pdf. You can request a copy by calling 410-576-7000.

The form included with this pamphlet does *not* give anyone power to handle your money. We do not have a standard form to send. Talk to your lawyer about planning for financial issues in case of incapacity.

Part II of the Advance Directive: Treatment Preferences ("Living Will")

You have the right to use an advance directive to say what you want about future life-sustaining treatment issues. You can do this in Part II of the form. If you both name a health care agent and make decisions about treatment in an advance directive, it's important that you say (in Part II, paragraph G) whether you want your agent to be strictly bound by whatever treatment decisions you make.

Part II is a living will. It lets you decide about life-sustaining procedures in three situations: when death from a terminal condition is imminent despite the application of life-sustaining procedures; a condition of permanent unconsciousness called a persistent vegetative state; and end-stage condition, which is an advanced, progressive, and incurable condition resulting in complete physical dependency. One example of end-stage condition could be advanced Alzheimer's disease.

1. *Must I use any particular form?*

No. An optional form is provided, but you may change it or use a different form altogether. Of course, no health care provider may deny you care simply because you decided not to fill out a form.

2. *Who can be picked as a health care agent?*

Anyone who is 18 or older except, in general, an owner, operator, or employee of a health care facility where a patient is receiving care.

3. *Who can witness an advance directive?*

Two witnesses are needed. Generally, any competent adult can be a witness, including your doctor or other health care provider (but be aware that some facilities have a policy against their employees serving as witnesses). If you name a health care agent, that person cannot be a witness for your advance directive. Also, **one** of the two witnesses must be someone who (i) will not receive money or property from your estate and (ii) is not the one you have named to handle your estate after your death.

4. *Do the forms have to be notarized?*

No, but if you travel frequently to another state, check with a knowledgeable lawyer to see if that state requires notarization.

5. *Do any of these documents deal with financial matters?*

No. If you want to plan for how financial matters can be handled if you lose capacity, talk with your lawyer.

6. *When using these forms to make a decision, how do I show the choices that I have made?*

Write your **initials** next to the statement that says what you want. **Don't** use checkmarks or X's. If you want, you can also draw lines all the way through other statements that do not say what you want.

7. *Should I fill out both Parts I and II of the advance directive form?*

It depends on what you want to do. If all you want to do is name a health care agent, just fill out Parts I and III, and talk to the person about how they should decide issues for you. If all you want to do is give treatment instructions, fill out Parts II and III. If you want to do both, fill out all three parts.

8. *Are these forms valid in another state?*

It depends on the law of the other state. Most state laws recognize advance directives made somewhere else.

9. *How can I get advance directive forms for another state?*

Contact the National Hospice and Palliative Care Organization (NHPCO) at 1-800-658-8898 or on the Internet at:
https://www.nhpco.org/patients-and-caregivers/advance-care-planning/advance-directives/downloading-your-states-advance-directive/

10. *To whom should I give copies of my advance directive?*

Give copies to your doctor, your health care agent and backup agent(s), hospital or nursing home if you will be staying there, and family members or friends who should know of your wishes. Consider carrying a card in your wallet saying you have an advance directive and who to contact.

11. *Does the federal law on medical records privacy (HIPAA) require special language about my health care agent?*

Special language is not required, but it is prudent. Language about HIPAA has been incorporated into the form.

12. *Can my health care agent or my family decide treatment issues differently from what I wrote?*

It depends on how much flexibility you want to give. Some people want to give family members or others flexibility in applying the living will. Other people want it followed very strictly. Say what you want in Part II, Paragraph G.

13. Is an advance directive the same as a "Patient's Plan of Care", "Instructions on Current Life-Sustaining Treatment Options" form, or Medical Orders for Life-Sustaining Treatment (MOLST) form?

No. These are forms used in health care facilities to document discussions about current life-sustaining treatment issues. These forms are not meant for use as anyone's advance directive. Instead, they are medical records, to be done only when a doctor or other health care professional presents and discusses the issues. A MOLST form contains medical orders regarding life-sustaining treatments relating to a patient's medical condition.

14. Can my doctor override my living will?

Usually, no. However, a doctor is not required to provide a "medically ineffective" treatment even if a living will asks for it.

15. If I have an advance directive, do I also need a MOLST form?

It depends. If you **don't** want emergency medical services personnel to try to resuscitate you in the event of cardiac or respiratory arrest, you must have a MOLST form containing a DNR order signed by your doctor. nurse practitioner, or physician assistant. A signed EMS/DNR order approved by the Maryland Institute for Emergency Medical Services Systems would also be valid.

16. Does the DNR Order have to be in a particular form?

Yes. Emergency medical services personnel have very little time to evaluate the situation and act appropriately. So, it is not practical to ask them to interpret documents that may vary in form and content. Instead, the standardized MOLST form has been developed. Have your doctor or health care facility visit the MOLST web site at http://marylandmolst.org or contact the Maryland Institute for Emergency Medical Services System at (410) 706-4367 to obtain information on the MOLST form.

17. Can I fill out a form to become an organ donor?

Yes, Use Part I of the "After My Death" form.

18. What about donating my body for medical education or research?

Part II of the "After My Death" form is a general statement of these wishes. The State Anatomy Board has a specific donation program, with a pre-registration form available. Call the Anatomy Board at 1-800-879-2728 for that form and additional information.

19. If I appoint a health care agent and the health care agent and any back-up agent dies or otherwise becomes unavailable, a surrogate decision maker may need to be consulted to make the same treatment decisions that my health care agent would have made. Is the surrogate decision maker required to follow my instructions given in the advance directive?

Yes, the surrogate decision maker is required to make treatment decisions based on your known wishes. An advance directive that contains clear and unambiguous instructions regarding treatment options is the best evidence of your known wishes and therefore must be honored by the surrogate decision maker.

Part II, paragraph G enables you to choose one of two options with regard to the degree of flexibility you wish to grant the person who will ultimately make treatment decisions for you, whether that person is a health care agent or a surrogate decision maker. Under the first option you would instruct the decision maker that your stated preferences are meant to guide the decision maker but may be departed from if the decision maker believes that doing so would be in your best interests. The second option requires the decision maker to follow your stated preferences strictly, even if the decision maker thinks some alternative would be better.

REVISED AUGUST 2019

vi

MARYLAND ADVANCE DIRECTIVE:
PLANNING FOR FUTURE HEALTH CARE DECISIONS

By: _______________________________________   **Date of Birth:** ___________________
        (Print Name)   (Month/Day/Year)

Using this advance directive form to do health care planning is completely optional. Other forms are also valid in Maryland. No matter what form you use, talk to your family and others close to you about your wishes.

This form has two parts to state your wishes, and a third part for needed signatures. Part I of this form lets you answer this question: If you cannot (or do not want to) make your own health care decisions, who do you want to make them for you? The person you pick is called your health care agent. **Make sure you talk to your health care agent (and any back-up agents) about this important role.** Part II lets you write your preferences about efforts to extend your life in three situations: terminal condition, persistent vegetative state, and end-stage condition. In addition to your health care planning decisions, you can choose to become an organ donor after your death by filling out the form for that too.

➔   You can fill out Parts I and II of this form, or only Part I, or only Part II. Use the form to reflect your wishes, then sign in front of two witnesses (Part III). If your wishes change, make a new advance directive.

Make sure you give a copy of the completed form to your health care agent, your doctor, and others who might need it. Keep a copy at home in a place where someone can get it if needed. Review what you have written periodically.

PART I: SELECTION OF HEALTH CARE AGENT

A. Selection of Primary Agent

I select the following individual as my agent to make health care decisions for me:

Name: ____

Address: ____

____

Telephone Numbers: ____
                                        (home and cell)

B. Selection of Back-up Agents
(Optional; form valid if left blank)

1. If my primary agent cannot be contacted in time or for any reason is unavailable or unable or unwilling to act as my agent, then I select the following person to act in this capacity:

Name: ____

Address: ____

____

Telephone Numbers: ____
(home and cell)

2. If my primary agent and my first back-up agent cannot be contacted in time or for any reason are unavailable or unable or unwilling to act as my agent, then I select the following person to act in this capacity:

Name: ____

Address: ____

____

Telephone Numbers: ____
(home and cell)

C. Powers and Rights of Health Care Agent

I want my agent to have full power to make health care decisions for me, including the power to:

1. Consent or not to medical procedures and treatments which my doctors offer, including things that are intended to keep me alive, like ventilators and feeding tubes;

2. Decide who my doctor and other health care providers should be; and

3. Decide where I should be treated, including whether I should be in a hospital, nursing home, other medical care facility, or hospice program.

4. I also want my agent to:

   a. Ride with me in an ambulance if ever I need to be rushed to the hospital; and

   b. Be able to visit me if I am in a hospital or any other health care facility.

THIS ADVANCE DIRECTIVE DOES NOT MAKE MY AGENT
RESPONSIBLE FOR ANY OF THE COSTS OF MY CARE.

This power is subject to the following conditions or limitations:
(Optional; form valid if left blank)

D. **How my Agent is to Decide Specific Issues**

I trust my agent's judgment. My agent should look first to see if there is anything in Part II of this advance directive that helps decide the issue. Then, my agent should think about the conversations we have had, my religious and other beliefs and values, my personality, and how I handled medical and other important issues in the past. If what I would decide is still unclear, then my agent is to make decisions for me that my agent believes are in my best interest. In doing so, my agent should consider the benefits, burdens, and risks of the choices presented by my doctors.

E. **People My Agent Should Consult**
(Optional; form valid if left blank)

In making important decisions on my behalf, I encourage my agent to consult with the following people. By filling this in, I do not intend to limit the number of people with whom my agent might want to consult or my agent's power to make decisions.

Name(s)   **Telephone Number(s):**

_______________________________   _______________________________

_______________________________   _______________________________

_______________________________   _______________________________

_______________________________   _______________________________

F. **In Case of Pregnancy**
(Optional, for women of child-bearing years only; form valid if left blank)

If I am pregnant, my agent shall follow these specific instructions:

G. Access to my Health Information – Federal Privacy Law (HIPAA) Authorization

1. If, prior to the time the person selected as my agent has power to act under this document, my doctor wants to discuss with that person my capacity to make my own health care decisions, I authorize my doctor to disclose protected health information which relates to that issue.

2. Once my agent has full power to act under this document, my agent may request, receive, and review any information, oral or written, regarding my physical or mental health, including, but not limited to, medical and hospital records and other protected health information, and consent to disclosure of this information.

3. For all purposes related to this document, my agent is my personal representative under the Health Insurance Portability and Accountability Act (HIPAA). My agent may sign, as my personal representative, any release forms or other HIPAA-related materials.

H. Effectiveness of this Part
(Read both of these statements carefully. Then, initial one only.)

My agent's power is in effect:

1. Immediately after I sign this document, subject to my right to make any decision about my health care if I want and am able to.
✎ ___________

>>OR<<

2. Whenever I am not able to make informed decisions about my health care, either because the doctor in charge of my care (attending physician) decides that I have lost this ability temporarily, or my attending physician and a consulting doctor agree that I have lost this ability **permanently**.
✎ ___________

> If the only thing you want to do is select a health care agent, skip Part II. Go to Part III to sign and have the advance directive witnessed. If you also want to write your treatment preferences, go to Part II. Also consider becoming an organ donor, using the separate form for that.

PART II: TREATMENT PREFERENCES ("LIVING WILL")

A. Statement of Goals and Values
(Optional: Form valid if left blank)

I want to say something about my goals and values, and especially what's most important to me during the last part of my life:

B. Preference in Case of Terminal Condition
(If you want to state what your preference is, initial **one** only. If you do not want to state a preference here, cross through the whole section.)

If my doctors certify that my death from a terminal condition is imminent, even if life-sustaining procedures are used:

1. Keep me comfortable and allow natural death to occur. I do not want any medical interventions used to try to extend my life. I do not want to receive nutrition and fluids by tube or other medical means.

    >>OR<<

2. Keep me comfortable and allow natural death to occur. I do not want medical interventions used to try to extend my life. If I am unable to take enough nourishment by mouth, however, I want to receive nutrition and fluids by tube or other medical means.

    >>OR<<

3. Try to extend my life for as long as possible, using all available interventions that in reasonable medical judgment would prevent or delay my death. If I am unable to take enough nourishment by mouth, I want to receive nutrition and fluids by tube or other medical means.

Page 5 of 8

C. **Preference in Case of Persistent Vegetative State**
(If you want to state what your preference is, initial **one** only. If you do not want to state a preference here, cross through the whole section.)

If my doctors certify that I am in a persistent vegetative state, that is, if I am not conscious and am not aware of myself or my environment or able to interact with others, and there is no reasonable expectation that I will ever regain consciousness:

1. Keep me comfortable and allow natural death to occur. I do not want any medical interventions used to try to extend my life. I do not want to receive nutrition and fluids by tube or other medical means.
⚖__________

   >>OR<<

2. Keep me comfortable and allow natural death to occur. I do not want medical interventions used to try to extend my life. If I am unable to take enough nourishment by mouth, however, I want to receive nutrition and fluids by tube or other medical means.
⚖__________

   >>OR<<

3. Try to extend my life for as long as possible, using all available interventions that in reasonable medical judgment would prevent or delay my death. If I am unable to take enough nourishment by mouth, I want to receive nutrition and fluids by tube or other medical means.
⚖__________

D. **Preference in Case of End-Stage Condition**
(If you want to state what your preference is, initial **one** only. If you do not want to state a preference here, cross through the whole section.)

If my doctors certify that I am in an end-stage condition, that is, an incurable condition that will continue in its course until death and that has already resulted in loss of capacity and complete physical dependency:

1. Keep me comfortable and allow natural death to occur. I do not want any medical interventions used to try to extend my life. I do not want to receive nutrition and fluids by tube or other medical means.
⚖__________

   >>OR<<

2. Keep me comfortable and allow natural death to occur. I do not want medical interventions used to try to extend my life. If I am unable to take enough nourishment by mouth, however, I want to receive nutrition and fluids by tube or other medical means.
⚖__________

   >>OR<<

3. Try to extend my life for as long as possible, using all available interventions that in reasonable medical judgment would prevent or delay my death. If I am unable to take enough nourishment by mouth, I want to receive nutrition and fluids by tube or other medical means.
⚖__________

27

E. Pain Relief

No matter what my condition, give me the medicine or other treatment I need to relieve pain.

F. In Case of Pregnancy
(Optional, for women of child-bearing years only; form valid if left blank)

If I am pregnant, my decision concerning life-sustaining procedures shall be modified as follows:

G. Effect of Stated Preferences
(Read both of these statements carefully. Then, initial **one** only.)

1. I realize I cannot foresee everything that might happen after I can no longer decide for myself. My stated preferences are meant to guide whoever is making decisions on my behalf and my health care providers, but I authorize them to be flexible in applying these statements if they feel that doing so would be in my best interest.

    ✎___________

    >>OR <<

2. I realize I cannot foresee everything that might happen after I can no longer decide for myself. Still, I want whoever is making decisions on my behalf and my health care providers to follow my stated preferences exactly as written, even if they think that some alternative is better.

    ✎___________

By signing below as the Declarant, I indicate that I am emotionally and mentally competent to make this advance directive and that I understand its purpose and effect. I also understand that this document replaces any similar advance directive I may have completed before this date.

____   _______________________________
(Signature of Declarant)   (Date)

The Declarant signed or acknowledged signing this document in my presence and, based upon personal observation, appears to be emotionally and mentally competent to make this advance directive.

____   _______________________________
(Signature of Witness)   (Date)

____
Telephone Number(s):

____   _______________________________
(Signature of Witness)   (Date)

____
Telephone Number(s):

(**Note:** Anyone selected as a health care agent in Part I may not be a witness. Also, at least one of the witnesses must be someone who will not knowingly inherit anything from the Declarant or otherwise knowingly gain a financial benefit from the Declarant's death. Maryland law does **not** require this document to be notarized.

AFTER MY DEATH

(This document is optional. Do only what reflects your wishes.)

By: ____ **Date of Birth:** ________________
(Print Name)   (Month/Day/Year)

PART I: ORGAN DONATION

(Initial the ones that you want. Cross through any that you do not want.)

Upon my death I wish to donate: ✍ _______________
Any needed organs, tissues, or eyes.   ✍ _______________

Only the following organs, tissues or eyes:

I authorize the use of my organs, tissues, or eyes:

For transplantation   ✍ _______________

For therapy   ✍ _______________

For research   ✍ _______________

For medical education   ✍ _______________

For any purpose authorized by law   ✍ _______________

I understand that no vital organ, tissue, or eye may be removed for transplantation until after I have been pronounced dead. *This document is not intended to change anything about my health care while I am still alive.* After death, I authorize any appropriate support measures to maintain the viability for transplantation of my organs, tissues, and eyes until organ, tissue, and eye recovery has been completed. I understand that my estate will not be charged for any costs related to this donation.

PART II: DONATION OF BODY

After any organ donation indicated in Part I, I wish my body to be donated for use in a medical study program.

✍ _______________

PART III: DISPOSITION OF BODY AND FUNERAL ARRANGEMENTS

I want the following person to make decisions about the disposition of my body and my funeral arrangements: (Either initial the first or fill in the second.)

The health care agent who I named in my advance directive.

>>OR<<

This person:

Name: ____

Address: ____

____

Telephone Number(s): ____
(Home and Cell)

If I have written my wishes below, they should be followed. If not, the person I have named should decide based on conversations we have had, my religious or other beliefs and values, my personality, and how I reacted to other peoples' funeral arrangements. My wishes about the disposition of my body and my funeral arrangements are:

PART IV: SIGNATURE AND WITNESSES

By signing below, I indicate that I am emotionally and mentally competent to make this donation and that I understand the purpose and effect of this document.

_______________________________   _______________________________
(Signature of Donor)   (Date)

The Donor signed or acknowledged signing the foregoing document in my presence and, based upon personal observation, appears to be emotionally and mentally competent to make this donation.

_______________________________   _______________________________
(Signature of Witness)   (Date)
____
Telephone Number(s):

_______________________________   _______________________________
(Signature of Witness)   (Date)
____
Telephone Number(s):

Page 2 of 2

31

AFTER MY DEATH

Part II: Donation of Body

The State Anatomy Board, a unit of the Department of Health administers a statewide Body Donation Program. Anatomical Donation allows individuals to dedicate the use of their bodies upon death to advance medical education, clinical and allied-health training and research study to Maryland's medical study institutions. The Anatomy Board requires individuals to pre-register prior to death as an anatomical donor to the state Body Donation Program. There are no medical restrictions or qualifications to becoming a "Body Donor". At death the Board will assume the custody and control of the body for study use. It is truly a legacy left behind for others to have healthier lives. For donation information and forms you can contact the Board toll-free at 800.879.2728

Did You Remember To ...

- ☐ Fill out Part I if you want to name a health care agent?

- ☐ Name one or two back-up agents in case your first choice as health care agent is not available when needed?

- ☐ Talk to your agents and back-up agent about your values and priorities, and decide whether that's enough guidance or whether you also want to make specific health care decisions in the advance directive?

- ☐ If you want to make specific decisions, fill out Part II, choosing carefully among alternatives?

- ☐ Sign and date the advance directive in Part III, in front of two witnesses who also need to sign?

- ☐ Look over the "After My Death" form to see if you want to fill out any part of it?

- ☐ Make sure your health care agent (if you named one), your family, and your doctor know about your advance care planning?

- ☐ Give a copy of your advance directive to your health care agent, family members, doctor, and hospital or nursing home if you are a patient there?

Advanced Directive Wallet Card

Would your doctor or family know where to find your Advance Health Care Directive or Living Will quickly if you were unable to tell them where it is?

An Advance Health Care Directive, which includes a Living Will, is only useful if it can be found and read when you are unable to make medical decisions for yourself. Typically, if you are unable to make medical decisions for yourself, you are not able to tell your doctor or your family where your Advance Directive is located. This is why the Attorney General's Office has developed a small card that you can keep in your wallet to document the location of your Advance Health Care Directive.

Two cards are provided. Just cut out a card, fill it in, fold it, and put it in your wallet or billfold.

These cards are not the same as a Do Not Resuscitate or DNR order.

If you want emergency medical services personnel to refrain from resuscitating you, you need a Maryland Medical Orders for Life-Sustaining Treatment (MOLST) form. That form has to be filled out by a physician or a nurse practitioner. Copies are available from the Maryland Institute for Emergency Medical Services Systems by calling 410-706-4367. You can also visit the website at www.marylandmolst.org and click on "MOLST Form."

For more information about Advance Health Care Directives, please visit the Attorney Gener-al's website at www.marylandattorneygeneral.gov and click on the button labeled Advance Directive/Living wills. You will find advance directive forms and instructions and other useful information, including the booklet: "Making Medical Decisions for Someone Else: A Guide for Marylanders" by clicking on "Guidance for Health Care Proxies." Copies of advance directive forms and instructions and the booklet can also be obtained by calling 410-576-7000.

ADVANCE HEALTH CARE DIRECTIVE

I HAVE AN ADVANCE DIRECTIVE.

My Name: _______________
My Physician's Name: _______________
Physician's Phone #: _______________

COPIES ARE HELD BY:

Name: _______________
Phone #s: _______________
____
(over)

OTHER COPIES ARE HELD BY:

Name: _______________
Phone #s: _______________
Name: _______________
Phone #s: _______________

I ALSO HAVE A HEALTH CARE AGENT.

Agent's Name: _______________
Phone #s: _______________
(over)

ADVANCE HEALTH CARE DIRECTIVE

I HAVE AN ADVANCE DIRECTIVE.

My Name: _______________
My Physician's Name: _______________
Physician's Phone #: _______________

COPIES ARE HELD BY:

Name: _______________
Phone #s: _______________
____
(over)

OTHER COPIES ARE HELD BY:

Name: _______________
Phone #s: _______________
Name: _______________
Phone #s: _______________

I ALSO HAVE A HEALTH CARE AGENT.

Agent's Name: _______________
Phone #s: _______________
(over)

<u>**Preparing to Complete Your Will Checklist**</u>

The following items and information may be needed to complete your will. Your Layer will have more specific information.

- ❏ **Documents:**
    - ❏ Birth certificates/ adoption paperwork of minor children
    - ❏ Real estate deeds
    - ❏ Vehicle titles
    - ❏ Checking account statement/ numbers
    - ❏ Savings account statement/ numbers
    - ❏ Money market account statement/ numbers
    - ❏ Insurance policy documents/ account numbers
    - ❏ Business accounts and insurance information
    - ❏ Funeral insurance or funeral expenses account documents
- ❏ **Existing debt:**
    - ❏ Mortgage
    - ❏ Home equity lines of credit
    - ❏ Student loans
    - ❏ Car loans
    - ❏ Other loans
    - ❏ Credit card debt
    - ❏ Medical bills
- ❏ **Information**
    - ❏ Full legal names, dates of birth, addresses and phone numbers for any beneficiaries
    - ❏ Social security numbers
    - ❏ List of legal/professional advisors and their contact information (lawyer, insurance agents, banker, investment agent, etc.)
    - ❏ List of debts
    - ❏ List of assets
        - ❏ List of bequests
- ❏ **Questions to answer**
    - ❏ Who will become the guardian for dependents?
    - ❏ Who will take in pets?
    - ❏ Who are your beneficiaries?
        - ❏ If beneficiaries die, who will the assets/estate pass to?
    - ❏ Who will be the Executor of the will?
        - ❏ Will you have a co-executor?
    - ❏ Who will be given Power of Attorney?

Guardian(s) for my dependents and their contact information:

Person(s) who will take care of my pet(s):

My Beneficiaries (Full names, addresses, birthdays, contact information):

My Beneficiaries (Full names, addresses, birthdays, contact information) con't:

Executor of my Will and their contact information:

Co- Executor of my Will and their contact information:

____

____

____

____

____

____

My Power of Attorney and their contact information:

____

____

____

____

____

____

Legal and professional advisors and their contact information:

____

____

____

____

____

____

____

____

____

Co- Executor of my Will and their contact information:

____

My debts:

____

____

____

____

____

____

____

____

____

____

____

____

My assets & bequests:

____

____

____

____

____

____

____

____

____

____

____

My assets & bequests continued:

My assets & bequests continued:

List of my accounts (account numbers, passcodes, pins, location of keys, etc.):

List of my accounts continued:

List of my accounts continued:

42

List of my accounts continued:

<u>**Other Notes/Information**</u>

44